Original title:
Floral Fragments

Author: Lila Davenport
ISBN HARDBACK: 978-1-80566-701-8
ISBN PAPERBACK: 978-1-80566-986-9

Fleeting Orchid Memories

In a pot, they stretch so high,
With little arms that wave goodbye.
They dreamed of dances, light and free,
Yet here they are, just leaves and me.

I watered them with hopes and sighs,
But orchids laugh in sly disguise.
Their petals fall like giggling sneezes,
While I compose my flower reasons.

Ghosts of Springtime Blooms

The daisies whispered life anew,
But ghosts of blooms, they bid adieu.
Petunia's wails, so loud, so bright,
Float through the air, then vanish at night.

Laughter echoes where tulips bled,
They once were pink, now look quite dead.
With garden gnomes that guard their rest,
I chuckle soft, they were the best.

Traces of Color in the Wind

A rainbow danced upon the breeze,
But petals drifted like old cheese.
Colors swirling, who can resist?
Yet they end up in a compost mist.

With every gust, they play and tease,
Catching laughter among the trees.
They paint the sky, then fade away,
Leaving just jokes for another day.

Disposable Gardens

I planted dreams in pots so cheap,
While wasting time, I drift to sleep.
The daisies laugh at my poor choice,
As weeds compete and raise their voice.

Each sip of sun, a hopeful glance,
Yet they decay, not left to chance.
A toss of petals, a fleeting chance,
My garden's done, they shan't advance.

The Language of Wilted Leaves

Leaves gossip in whispers,
Drooping low, laughing hard.
They speak of sunlit breezes,
And cat's paws in the yard.

An awkward dance they do,
Twirling down from the trees.
"I'm not giving up!" they shout,
As squirrels munch on their leaves.

A picnic for the ants,
Underneath a bending vine.
"Watch your toes!" they warn each other,
"This ground is shot and fine!"

The dance ends with a sigh,
As autumn takes a bow.
With smiley faces on the ground,
They dream of springtime now.

Shattered Stems

Oh, those stems! What a crew,
Bending in a funny way.
One just tripped on a root,
And rolled down into the hay.

Petal pals are laughing loud,
While dusting off their clothes.
"At least I'm not a weed!" one shouts,
As another strikes a pose.

They joke about their faults,
And blemishes that they hold.
"My stem is proud and tall!"
Said the one who feels quite old.

Shattered dreams weave laughter bright,
In the garden's sunny spot.
Even in their brokenness,
They're charming, like they're not.

Echoes of a Withering Rose

In the corner of the pot,
A rose whispers, "I'm not done!"
With petals curling softly,
It plots its next great pun.

"Unfurl me!" cries another,
As if they'll steal the show.
But down below, the roots just giggle,
In their secret, silent tow.

"Oh no, you can't out-shimmer,"
One laughs and starts to sway.
'Last bloom standing' bets are on,
On who's going out today!

The petals float like gossip,
In this garden party space.
With every wilt, they sparkle,
Dancing on, just in grace.

Petals and Shadows

A petal slipped on purpose,
In a shadow's playful dance.
"Catch me if you can!" it cried,
Giving sunshine a chance.

Tiny webs of laughter spun,
From the flowers growing bold.
“Don’t let that shadow get you!”
Said the marigold with gold.

In mischievous delight,
They swayed beneath the moon.
A game of hide and seek began,
In a garden sweet as June.

As shadows crept and gleamed,
The petals twirled in glee.
For life’s a jolly jest, they say,
With giggles, soft and free.

Daisies in Dusk's Embrace

Daisies wink in twilight's glow,
Their petals whisper secrets low.
Jokes ensue in the fading light,
As they giggle through the night.

Bumblebees with hats ask who,
Dance around like it's a zoo.
'Why so serious?' the daisies tease,
'Just chill and sway with the evening breeze.'

The Art of Nature's Palette

Painting buds with colors bright,
Nature's brush in pure delight.
A rogue tulip splats on a wall,
As violets giggle, 'Look at that fall!'

Pansies pout with a sassy flair,
While sunflowers strut without a care.
'Your paint's outside the lines!' they yell,
But blooms don’t mind, they love their spell.

Serenade of Wildflowers

Wildflowers sing a cheeky tune,
Under the gaze of a blushing moon.
'Nobody calls us weeds!' they shout,
'Join the party, don’t sit out!'

With the crickets as their band,
The daisies clap, all hand in hand.
'Nature’s show, a riotous spree,
Who knew growing could be so free?'

Shadows of a Sunflower's Smile

In shadows cast by sunflowers tall,
They chuckle and whisper, having a ball.
'Got a secret?', asks a daisy so sly,
'Only if you spin like us and fly!'

Oh, how they sway, in silly dances,
Chasing the wind, taking chances.
With laughter bubbling like morning dew,
'We’re towering giants! How 'bout you?'

Tattered Blooms

Petals dance in swirling air,
Whispering secrets without a care.
A daisy playing hide and seek,
Declares, 'I’m not too chic!'

Sunflowers wearing sunglasses wide,
Think they’re too cool for the garden's ride.
Roses roll their eyes, you see,
‘Glamour isn’t guaranteed!’

Hues of Forgotten Summers

Once bright hues now faded dreams,
In corners where the sunlight beams.
Lavender giggles at its state,
'Please, don't call me second-rate!'

Chives dressed up in purple hats,
Mocking the sleeping sleepy rats.
'Our colors may be past their prime,
But hey, we’ve still got a rhyme!'

The Last Sigh of Cherry Blossoms

As blossoms fall in a gentle flurry,
They croon of love, but oh, what a hurry!
'Last chance for selfies!' they call,
Before they trip and start to sprawl.

A bee buzzes with sweet delight,
Stuck in a petal, oh, what a sight!
'Stop horsing around, let's make a toast!'
Says a dazed flower, almost a ghost.

Unraveled Nature's Palette

Splatters of paint across the lawn,
A tulip yawns at the break of dawn.
'Who spilled my color? It's not right!'
Fuming wisteria, ready to fight.

Dandelions blow puffs of air,
Laughing together, debonair.
'Our colors clash, but who really cares?
We'll still shine bright, amidst the flares!'

In the Company of Florets

In a garden bright and spry,
The daisies dance, oh my, oh my!
With petals wide, they twirl and spin,
While bees just laugh, saying, "Let's begin!"

Pansies wear their silly frowns,
They giggle loud in bustling towns.
"Oh look at us!" the tulips shout,
"We've got the best bloom, no doubt!"

The roses boast of scents divine,
While violets snooze, feeling just fine.
"Can you believe what grows below?"
Said the weeds, "We're the stars of the show!"

So in this patch of petal fun,
Each flower shines, they're never done.
A comedy, this garden scene,
Where every bud is a laughing queen!

The Quiet Artist's Garden

In a nook where colors blend,
A painter insect likes to mend.
With brush of pollen on his wing,
He strokes the flowers, and they sing!

The lilies pose, all calm and neat,
While butterflies just skip a beat.
"Come on, bloom, it's time to shine!
Let's make this garden look divine!"

The daisies laugh, they shout, "Encore!"
"Let's act like we're not bored anymore!"
As petals flail and come to life,
They forget all about petty strife!

With splashes bright on canvas green,
Each blossom giggles, art unseen.
A gallery of joyful glee,
Where nature's brush sets spirits free!

Reverie in the Rosewood

In rosewood shade, a dream unfolds,
With whispers soft as tales of old.
A snail in boots, oh what a sight!
He saunters slow, yet feels so bright!

The tulip crowns a wobbly snail,
While crickets sing a silly tale.
“Oh please, do hurry!” petals pray,
As dew drops laugh, they sway and play!

Bumblebees buzz with much delight,
In dance-offs held beneath the light.
“Who’s the best? Oh, what a joke!”
Petals chuckle, “We’re all bespoke!”

In the wood, where flowers tease,
A whimsical ball with rustling leaves.
Each moment blooms with joyful cheer,
For nature’s whimsy draws us near!

The Essence of a Garden's Heart

In the heart of blooms, loud laughs erupt,
With daisies gossiping and irises jumped.
"Oh darling, can you see the bees?
They're forgetting how to say 'cheese!'"

The sunflowers stretch, tall and grand,
While tulips giggle, hand in hand.
"I can whisper sweeter than you,
But let's not argue—let's just bloom!"

A prickly thorn, he claims the crown,
Yet every flower wears a frown.
"Not this guy," the daisies chime,
"Let's skip the thorn and have a rhyme!"

So in this garden, joy awakes,
With playful pranks and gentle flake.
Each petal tells a funny part,
The humor sewn into nature's heart!

Where the Violets Whisper

In a garden of giggles, the violets play,
Tickling the tulips with laughter all day.
Petals in pajamas, they twirl and spin,
Whispering secrets of the chaos within.

The bees are the bouncers, they dance with flair,
Buzzing to rhythms, with pollen to share.
Daisies do dabble in gossip and cheer,
Chasing the daisies, what mischief is near!

Scent of the Invisible

A scent drifts by on a breezy whim,
Invisible blooms on a light-hearted whim.
The roses just giggle at the daffodils,
Who claim they're the stars with the brightest skills.

With whispers of mint and a joke from the air,
The daisies will dance, just without a care.
Petunias cracking up at the peonies' jokes,
In a world of perfume, where laughter provokes.

The Heartbeat of Hibiscus

Hibiscus wears shades, all ready to strut,
With flowers on his head, he's quite the nut.
Boasting his colors, oh what a show!
He claims he could outshine the rainbow's glow.

The sunflowers chuckle, with heads held up high,
As hibiscus' stories just make them all sigh.
"Look at me, I'm vibrant!" he shouts to the rye,
While daisies just snicker as bees pass them by.

In the Arms of a Daisy

In the arms of a daisy, all cozy and bright,
Butterflies gather for a giggling night.
The moonbeam is laughing, they dance with delight,
A chorus of petals makes everything light.

With jests from the lilacs, and puns from the ferns,
The daisies keep swaying, waiting for turns.
"Who's the prettiest?" bellowed, the peonies call,
"In the garden of whimsy, we're all having a ball!"

Memories in Lavender Hues

In the garden where giggles bloom,
Lavender whispers, casting a room.
Bee-bumbles tickle a petal's soft skin,
Tickling flowers, let the laughter begin.

Socks on the line, a lavender dance,
Honeybees plotting a silly romance.
Winking at daisies, they all conspire,
To blow pink bubbles, the garden's attire.

A windstorm knocks over the tulip parade,
Petals in laughter, a clumsy charade.
Lavender's scent, with a dash of glee,
Turns everyday moments to bright jubilee.

Each stem a tale of a mischief done,
With giggling flowers, they shine like the sun.
Memories wrapped in a lavender hue,
Weaving the funny in breezes so true.

Hues of Hope in Petal Form

In a meadow of dreams, colors collide,
Petals in hula hula, dancing with pride.
Wishing on daisies, a comical sight,
They toss up their hopes, taking off in flight.

But oh! A sly gust steals their big chance,
Petals on the move in an awkward dance.
Dandelions chuckling, they scatter like fries,
Wishes fly wild, like birds in disguise.

Butterflies giggle, wearing shades of flair,
With each flap and flutter, they just do not care.
Paintbrush petals, a canvas so bright,
Hope rolls out laughing, embracing the light.

When blooms start to fade, they don't shed a tear,
Instead, they burst forth with a floral cheer.
In the hues of hope, all spirits conform,
Each petal a jest, a vibrant new norm.

The Dance of the Marigold

With a wiggle and giggle, marigolds sway,
Sunbeams in petals, they frolic and play.
Chasing the shadows with bright orange glee,
Saying, "We're here for a laugh, not to flee!"

A waltz with the daisies, a twirl with the grass,
Marigolds chat with snails passing en masse.
Bouncing like beans, with stories to spill,
Each flower a joker, with laughter to fill.

Twirling in circles, their colors unite,
The garden a stage in the soft, golden light.
With every child's giggle, the blooms twist and whirl,
In the dance of the marigold, joy starts to unfurl.

Then comes a tumble, a splash of bright hue,
Splat! A petal lands on a poor ladybug's shoe.
Yet in the mess, they find something bold,
Laughter's the treasure; it never grows old.

Raindrops on Rose Leaves

Caught in a giggle, the raindrops rejoice,
Slipping and sliding with a tiny, sweet voice.
They dance on the rose leaves, all shiny and round,
Each droplet a chuckle, a jubilant sound.

Oh, look at the petals, like umbrellas they bloom,
Catching the laughter, dispelling the gloom.
Raindrops in rhythm, a soft little tap,
Turning the garden to a splashy fun map.

The roses, they wobble, in tremors of cheer,
"Watch us! We're spinning!" they yell, so sincere.
Together they shimmer, like stars in a torrent,
Playing on petals, it's a loving current.

Through puddles of giggles, they bounce and they hop,
Creating a symphony that never will stop.
With each little splash, they grow bolder, it's true,
In raindrops on leaves, their laughter rings through.

A Bouquet of Secrets

In the garden, whispers bloom,
Petals giggle, scents assume.
Bees wear hats, they dance and spin,
Twirling secrets, laughter's kin.

Roses thread with tales so bright,
Tulips tell of a lost kite.
Daisies chuckle at the rain,
While violets gossip of a bane.

Sunflowers grin with sunlit glee,
As daisies wink, 'Come dance with me!'
Each stem holds a tale to share,
Nature's jesters, everywhere.

In this bouquet of blushing hues,
They mix their tales like sassy stews.
Pluck one secret, what a sight,
A funny world, both day and night.

The Art of Nature's Decay

Leaves speak in russet sighs,
Mushrooms giggle, no disguise.
Each twig tells of a broken dream,
Insects share tales in rhymed theme.

Flowers fade with a chuckled sigh,
Hello, goodbye, just passing by.
Ripe fruit drops, it's such a show,
Nature's humor in ebb and flow.

Petals down, they spin and whirl,
Creating laughter in a twirl.
The art of decay, what a sight,
A comedy in soft twilight.

So gather round to watch them teem,
Nature laughs, it’s quite the dream!
In wilting whispers, joy will stay,
In each end, a joke at play.

Mosaic of Wildflowers

A patchwork quilt of color bright,
Poppies giggle, what a sight!
Dandelions puff with pride,
Nature's clowns, they won't abide.

Buttercups play hopscotch fair,
With daisies dancing everywhere.
Lilies flaunt their polka dots,
In wildflower games, they tie their knots.

Each bloom shouts, 'Look at me!'
While sunbeams twirl in glee.
Jasmines whisper sweet delight,
As bees hold court in golden light.

This mosaic sings of cheer,
Petals laughing, bright and clear.
In every patch, a jolly face,
A garden party, a happy space.

Remnants of Sunlit Meadows

In sunlit fields where laughter sways,
Grasshoppers jump, a merry craze.
Wildflowers dance without a care,
Their laughter floats upon the air.

Butterfly jokes take flight with grace,
As blooms pose in a hilarious race.
Each stem leans, a strong contender,
In nature's games, a true sprender.

The sunbeams play peekaboo light,
While bumbles hum in sheer delight.
They share the punchlines, loud and clear,
Bringing joy, the meadow's cheer.

So wander through this jolly land,
Where petals giggle, hand in hand.
In each corner, a smile will sprout,
Remnants of laughter, there's no doubt.

Colors of a Wandering Heart

A daisy told a joke to me,
About a bee who drank too much tea.
He buzzed and stumbled, what a sight,
And danced with tulips all night bright.

The roses laughed, their petals flared,
"Dear grass, don't worry, we've all dared."
The violets chimed in, cheeky and spry,
"Just don't forget to wave goodbye!"

Sunflowers tilted, with a grin so wide,
"Why did the gardener go outside?"
"To plant some seeds, for laughs and cheer,
And tell his plants they're all sincere!"

In shades of pink and yellow hues,
The petals shared their silly views.
A wandering heart, lost in bloom,
Found laughter in nature's quirky room.

The Secret Song of the Seasons

Autumn leaves did a jig one day,
Chasing squirrels in a funny way.
They twirled and spun, with colors bright,
Singing softly into the night.

Winter whispered to a frosty bud,
"Wanna play, or just sit in the mud?"
The snowflakes giggled, a comical crew,
As icicles swayed, they knew what to do.

Spring yelled, "Let's have a jumping race!"
But daisies tripped, fell flat on their face.
While sunbeams chuckled from their perch high,
"All seasons unite, don't be shy!"

Summer shined with a glistening glee,
As bees hived in a harmony spree.
In this secret song, a tune we find,
The humor of nature, laughter entwined.

Tales Written in Petal Ink

Once a petal passed a funny note,
About a tree who learned to gloat.
"I'm taller than all, just look at me!"
But the grass whispered, "You're just a tree!"

A little bud laughed, "I'm shy today,
But wait until I bloom and sway!"
The daisies booed as they formed a line,
"Don't be shy, your time will shine!"

A garden party, wild and free,
With pansies dancing, a sight to see!
They wiggled and giggled, oh what a sight,
As the wind sang tunes in pure delight.

The sun joined in, with a cheerful wink,
"Let's write our tales with petal ink!"
In laughter and joy, they lay on the ground,
With stories of bloom, their fun knows no bound.

A Symphony of Stem and Seed

In gardens where the plants conspire,
The daisies dance, the weeds retire.
A trumpet sound from leafy greens,
The broccoli plays in veggie scenes.

The roses laugh with petal pride,
While daisies shove their heads outside.
It’s a concert full of quirky cheer,
Where every bloom plays loud and clear.

A cabbage sings a merry tune,
Chasing away the dull afternoon.
With carrots tapping to the beat,
Every veggie just can't be beat.

And as the sun begins to fade,
The flowers giggle, unafraid.
Each stem a part of nature’s skit,
In this grand garden, a perfect fit.

Transience of Tulips

The tulips blush in morning light,
Their colors bold, a cheerful sight.
But wait, oh dear, what's that I see?
A petal drop, just wait for me!

A breeze comes in, a quick attack,
Lopsided blooms begin to crack.
The tulip's dance is quite the show,
As petals wave, then down they go.

They try to hold their heads up high,
But gravity is sly and spry.
A tulip tumbles, oh so clumsy,
Yet still looks lovely, quite so funny.

In fields of blooms, they all unite,
A fleeting joy, a vivid sight.
They whisper secrets to the bee,
About their lives and what will be.

The Beauty Beneath Thorned Roses

There once were roses, bold and bright,
With thorny crowns that gave a fright.
Yet underneath their prickly guise,
Lay humor wrapped in sweet surprise.

A bumblebee dressed in a suit,
Buzzed past the thorns, without a hoot.
He feasted on nectar, without dread,
Sipped from the blooms, while petals shed.

The thorns complained, 'We're misunderstood!'
But blooms just winked, 'Oh, life is good!'
A game of tag in the floral way,
Roses at play, brightening the day.

So if you see those thorns up tall,
Remember they have charm, after all.
For beauty blooms in every case,
Even with pricks, there's time to embrace.

Woven in the Weeds

Among the weeds, the fun begins,
With grasses kicking tiny sins.
A dandelion, bold and free,
Proclaims itself a majesty!

The clover laughs, 'You think you're grand?'
While tiny bugs all take their stand.
They host a tea party on the patch,
With herb and leaf, oh what a catch!

A rogue snail slides in with grace,
Bringing shells for a wild embrace.
And all around, the laughter flows,
As garden chaos cheerfully grows.

So here's to weeds, both wild and proud,
They twist and twirl, they sing out loud.
In tangled joy, they weave their tale,
In nature's frame, they will prevail.

When Botanicals Fade

Petals fall like forgotten socks,
The garden's now a jumbled box.
Roses blushing, once so spry,
Now look like they've just said goodbye.

The daisies dance on wobbly stalks,
A waltz of wilt where no one talks.
The tulips pout, they just can't cope,
It's hard to bloom without some hope.

Sunshine giggles at the scene,
"Who knew plants could be so mean?"
A daffodil, with quite the flair,
Says, "I'm just looking for fresh air!"

So here we laugh at wilt and wane,
Eager for the next spring rain.
For every wilted, sad bouquet,
A chuckle makes it all okay.

Unseen Beauty in the Grass

In the grass, the weeds hold court,
Where dandelions come with sport.
They boast of beauty, wild and free,
Yet moms just call them ‘pests,’ you see!

Clover winks with a leafy grin,
“Find me a coin, let’s spin to win!”
While ants stage plays with crumbs and laughs,
They plot their next great heist with staffs.

A ladybug gives a sassy pose,
Saying, “Sleek? Honey, I’m just prose!”
The grasshoppers leap with such sweet glee,
Singing ballads of grass-filled spree.

So here we sit, beneath the sky,
With nature's quirks, we can’t deny.
In every blade, a story hums,
While laughter in the meadow thrums.

Soliloquy of Lilies

The lilies sigh in soft ballet,
“Do we twirl or just decay?”
With petals grand, they strut about,
While bees engage in buzzing shout.

“Have you heard?” a lily confides,
“Yesterday, we nearly cried!”
“But darling,” says her friend so bold,
“We’re fabulous, just look at our gold!”

In a garden gossip fair,
They tease the roses, unaware.
“Your thorns may keep you out of reach,
But we’re the stars; we’re quite the peach!”

As twilight dances in the light,
The lilies laugh away their fright.
For in the hush, they find their spark,
Winking shyly in the dark.

Sunsets on Dying Petals

When sunsets paint the petals red,
They laugh and say, "We're not yet dead!"
A vibrant glow in fading grace,
A wink of mischief, just in case.

"Oh darling sun, don't you be shy,
We're only fading to say goodbye!"
With silly spirit, they dance with glee,
"Tomorrow's blooms will sprout, you'll see!"

Even in the dusk so sweet,
Petals form a retro beat.
They chirp of glory, pasts well spent,
In every droop, there's still content.

So let's not mourn the withering hue,
For life's a jest, and laughs ensue.
With every sunset comes a chance,
To find joy in the wilted dance.

Petals That Speak

In the garden, petals chatter,
Gossiping blooms on a sunny platter.
Bees eavesdrop with buzzing delight,
While daisies debate through day and night.

Roses roll their eyes, oh what a scene,
Tulips tell jokes, they're quite the keen.
Lilies laugh, swinging their long, green legs,
While pansies play pranks on neighboring pegs.

Sunflowers boast of their height and pride,
Violets giggle, unable to hide.
Petals in laughter, it's quite absurd,
Nature's own comedy, never deterred.

So let's toast with nectar, raise a swift cheer,
To blossoms that banter, we hold so dear.
In a world of petals witty and spry,
Who knew plants could be so sly?

The Whispering Meadow

In a meadow where whispers abound,
Grass blades bend low, secrets are found.
Daffodils dance to a giggly tune,
While butterflies flutter beneath the moon.

Dandelions make wishes with a puff,
Saying, 'Life's short, let's have some fun, huh?'
The daisies nod, with their white little heads,
While crickets tap dance on all of their beds.

Gentle breezes tickle the bloom’s ear,
'Have you heard the news? The sun's finally here!'
They gossip and chortle, what a funny sight,
A meadow full of joy, oh what pure delight.

So waltz through the green, laugh without care,
For laughter in blossoms is quite rare,
A meadow's a theater, so don’t be late,
Join in the fun, it’s a buzzing fate!

Wonders of Nature's Canopy

Under the trees, where mischief abounds,
A canopy whispers in giggles and sounds.
Leaves play charades, their shadows will tease,
While squirrels enact their acorn adventures with ease.

Branches are lockers for secrets untold,
They chuckle together, both young and old.
A cocoon is a mystery, hark! Let's explore,
What if it's Santa, or a dragon galore?

In the rustle of leaves, jokes take their flight,
While petals conspire to brighten the night.
A tadpole tells tales that are wildly untrue,
About a frog prince dressed in bright blue.

So swing with the branches, let laughter ignite,
For nature's a canvas, a funny delight.
Beneath this grand canopy, let's all partake,
In wonders of laughter, make no mistake!

Moments Lost in Gardenia

In a garden of whims, the gardenias grin,
With noble fragrances that nudge you within.
They whisper of moments, both funny and sweet,
Of baking with butter, just don't use your feet!

A bee buzzes in, recounts a blunder,
Singing of flowers that laugh so much under.
Mint and basil rolling, tucked in a stew,
Finding fine spices just didn't break through.

Petunias critique the latest bloom style,
"I'll see you on Insta, just wait for a while!"
While lilacs update their 'fashion on stems',
It's a riot of colors, oh what silly gems!

In moments lost, where giggles blend in,
Gardenias dance, let the fun never thin.
So come join the laughter, a bloom can't be shy,
In this garden of giggles, just stop by!

Stray Seeds and Secrets

In a garden where no rules abide,
A sunflower tried to hide its pride.
It whispered tales of love and cheer,
To dandelions blowing far and near.

A rogue radish wore a vibrant hat,
Challenging peas to a dance-off chat.
They twirled and spun, quite out of tune,
While carrots laughed beneath the moon.

But behind the leaves, a secret stayed,
A ladybug lost in the parade.
She tripped on petals, quite a sight,
Claiming, "I prefer a quiet night!"

Yet as the veggies squeezed in tight,
They all agreed, this felt just right.
In a garden of jests, delight unfurled,
Sprouting giggles in their silly world.

Berries Under Blossoms

Beneath pink blooms, berries conspired,
To host a party, their hopes inspired.
Raspberry wore a crown of leaves,
While blueberry bubbled with sparkling thieves.

With cherry on top, they sang a tune,
Inviting all in the warm afternoon.
But as they danced, a squirrel did crash,
Spilling juice with a mighty splash!

The strawberries giggled, so ripe and bold,
"Let's feast on chaos, it never gets old!"
They sip on nectar, a tangy toast,
To the mishaps they love, they cherish the most.

And under green canopies, shadows writhe,
With laughter and sweetness, the berries thrive.
For in every stain, a story's sewn,
A berry bash where silliness is grown.

Fading Echoes of the Iris

In twilight hues, an iris sighed,
Complaining softly of petals fried.
"Once so vibrant, look at me now!
I've wilted faster than a lazy cow!"

Bumblebees buzzed, they had a plan,
To cheer her up, a lively fan.
"We'll paint you bright with pollen dust,
And you'll be fierce! Just build the rust!"

But the iris chuckled, a giggly tease,
"Please, do that and I'll sneeze with ease!"
They laughed together, a bloom belief,
Finding joy in fading, not just grief.

In gardens where shadows twist and bend,
A fading bloom can still make friends.
In every petal that drifts away,
Laughter lives on, come what may!

The Language of Fragrance

In the meadow where scents collide,
A lavender lured bees to confide.
It buzzed about how chic it smelled,
While daisies blushed, their secrets swelled.

A rose piped up with a sultry wink,
"Let's talk about musk and sweetened ink!"
Geraniums giggled, their scent a tease,
"Your charm's no match for my easy breeze!"

The violets chimed in, just a tad shy,
"Do we smell sweet, or just like pie?"
They all erupted in fragrant flair,
With each aroma, giggles filled the air.

So in this garden of scented grace,
Every perfume finds its place.
With each little whiff that takes a chance,
They share a language wrapped in dance.

The Thrill of Delicate Things

Tiny petals spin and twirl,
As I chase them round the whirl.
A sneeze disrupts my gentle dance,
Leaves me swatting in a trance.

Pollen floats like playful dust,
Insisting that I simply trust.
In summer's glow, I take a leap,
Oops! My allergies make me weep.

Daisies giggle in their patch,
While bees around me start to hatch.
I trip on roots, they laugh aloud,
Nature's mischief feels so proud.

If laughter blooms in every stem,
Then call me Queen of Whimsy's gem.
For forward I will always spring,
With silly joy in everything.

Verse in the Violets

In violets deep, a riddle's spun,
I think I've found a flowered fun.
Their purple hues, a hoot they bring,
Do they hum? I ask, if insects sing.

One violet whispered, 'Cheer up, mate!'+
While others joined; they couldn't wait.
A wreath of giggles round my head,
"If you can't play, now go to bed!"

A butterfly struts, such pomp and flair,
All while the violets stop and stare.
"Who's that joker?"—a petal exclaims,
"Just another one playing flowery games!"

So here I sit, among the crew,
In merriment, just me and you.
Eavesdropping on blooms, it's hard to tell,
What's truth or jest in this floral swell.

Soliloquy of the Snapdragon

Oh snapdragon, strong and bright,
Do you know you're quite a sight?
You chatter so in cheeky tongues,
While nearby, jolly laughter hums.

"Open wide!" you seem to say,
Spouting tales throughout the day.
I wish I had such flair to boast,
But I just sit and stare, engrossed.

Frogs in the shade share tiny jokes,
While ants march by in haughty pokes.
"Isn't it grand?" the blossoms sing,
But snapdragons steal the whole darn thing!

A dance recital with earthy ties,
Each snapdragon leaps, no need for lies.
A glorious show of color and glee,
Oh, how I'd love their giggle spree!

The Story of a Single Bloom

Once there was a bloom so shy,
In a garden's corner, by and by.
"Am I too small? Can I stand tall?"
It whispered soft, a hopeful call.

Sunshine beamed and dew drops laughed,
Being overlooked felt quite daft.
Passersby glanced, then blinked quick,
But beneath, it grew, oh what a trick!

One day a squirrel stopped by to perch,
"Hey little friend, you're quite the search!"
With laughter shared, they spun and played,
An unlikely bond that would not fade.

From tiny seed, a friendship bloomed,
In laughter's glow, their colors loomed.
The story of a single sprout,
Turns shy to bold, with cheerful shout!

Garden of Nightfall

In the dusk where daisies yawn,
A sleepy bee has lost its brawn.
It buzzes past, then hits a rose,
And off it tumbles, oh, who knows?

The moonlight laughs with every petal,
A snail's slow race, it takes a medal.
The tulips gossip, oh so sly,
About the bee that can’t quite fly.

The crickets chirp a funny tune,
While sunflowers slouch, like late afternoon.
It’s a garden of giggles, what a sight!
Where flowers dance under the moonlight.

At garden gates, the frogs debate,
If hopping's better than being late.
With pokey thorns and soft, soft leaves,
Who knew a garden could be such a tease?

The Quietude of Petal Showers

Petals drift like laughter in the air,
Dancing wildly without a care.
A squirrel slips, then strikes a pose,
While daisies snicker, whoa, look at those!

In showers soft, the colors gleam,
A butterfly lost, still chasing its dream.
The roses giggle with every breeze,
While daisies roll their eyes in tease.

A robin's tune is slightly off,
He chirps a note, then does he scoff.
The tulips droop in blush and cheer,
At every mishap, they hoot and sneer.

The fragrance mingles, sweet and bold,
A bee sneezes — heavens, it's gold!
In this quiet, a ruckus appears,
With every petal falls, a burst of cheers.

The Embrace of Fading Ferns

Where ferns curl like a sleeping cat,
A ladybug wore a tiny hat.
It stumbled down, a little clumsy,
In the ferns, oh, how it feels so funny!

The shadows play a game of hide,
As flowers laugh, they can't abide.
A bumblebee trips on its own wing,
And the ferns all chuckle, it's quite the thing.

With colors dimming, a spark of mirth,
The fading leaves discuss their worth.
An acorn quips, as wise as can be,
"Just wait until it's my turn to see!"

In this silent world of green delight,
The plants snicker at the fading light.
Though fading ferns want to snooze,
They still find time to share some views.

Sunlight Between the Blooms

Sunlight tumbles, laughter in rays,
Where flowers wiggle in sunny displays.
A bee in sunglasses feels so fly,
While daisies peek and wonder why.

Beneath the blooms, a rabbit plots,
A secret dance but not a lot.
He hops, he skips, he twirls just right,
Then tumbles hard, oh, what a sight!

The marigolds cheer with golden voices,
While petunias tease, making odd choices.
In the breeze, they gossip and swoon,
About a flower that thinks it's a balloon.

Sunlight glinting, laughter spills,
Where petals chatter, joy fulfills.
In this bumble of bloom and cheer,
Every laugh is music to the ear.

The Language of Lilies

In a meadow, lilies sway,
Chatting secrets of the day.
One says, 'Did you hear that bee?
He's been buzzing endlessly!'

Their petals wink like stars at night,
Whispering jokes in soft twilight.
'Why did the tulip cross the lane?
To get to the garden's funny vein!'

Daisies giggle, roses blush,
As nature's laughter starts to rush.
'Be careful, dear, the rain might spill,
And wash away your funny thrill!'

So amid the laughter and the cheer,
Lilies banter till spring's end is near.
Their petals burst with joy like glee,
A floral comedy, pure jubilee!

Fragrance of Forgotten Gardens

In gardens lost to time and space,
Forgotten blooms have found their place.
They tell tales of laughter long past,
Of bees that danced and pollen cast.

A daffodil with quirky style,
Sways to the breeze, a cheeky smile.
'Why don’t we ever get a guest?
It’s the weeds, they’re such a pest!'

Violets burst forth with giggles sly,
'Have you seen the daisies? Oh my!
They wear sunglasses just to pose,
While the shy pansies hide their woes!'

The fragrance swirls, a funny tune,
A scent of laughter 'neath the moon.
In forgotten gardens, pranks unfold,
Where nature’s humor never grows old!

Secrets in the Bougainvillea

The bougainvillea stands so bold,
With secrets in its petals told.
One shade whispers to another hue,
'Can you believe what blossoms do?'

They plot to tease the hapless sun,
Hiding from rays, oh what fun!
'Let’s pretend we're just a vine,
And wait for the sun to cross the line!'

Its vibrant colors claim the day,
But laughter hides just out of sway.
'Can a flower really have a cheer?
Of course! Just look, we have no fear!'

In the chaos of colors bright,
Bougainvillea revels in the light.
A tapestry of jokes and zest,
Where petals jest and never rest!

The Tapestry of Tiny Blooms

In a patch where tiny blooms align,
They giggle softly, intertwine.
'Have you met the cute little sprout?
He thinks he’s a tree, oh what a clout!'

The forget-me-nots keep their cool,
Remaining wise in this flowery school.
'Be sure to never take a fall,
For daisies are known to start a brawl!'

With petals small and tricks galore,
Each bloom awaits for laughter’s score.
'Let’s plan a prank on the big roses,
Hide their thorns with some silly poses!'

The tapestry weaves with joy and jest,
Tiny blooms put humor to the test.
In every nook, their giggles loom,
A riotous cheer among the bloom!

The Rhapsody of Blossoming

In a garden so bright, bees take flight,
Chasing scents in the morning light.
Roses gossip in shades of red,
While daisies laugh, 'We're not so fed!'

Tulips twirl in the gentle breeze,
Claiming they're the stars of the trees.
With every bloom, a tale unfolds,
Of petals and puns, oh so bold!

Sunflowers take selfies, posing tall,
While violets whisper, 'We're not that small!'
Pansies jest, saying, 'Life's a show,'
And marigolds clap, 'Come on, let’s go!'

In this lively dance, oh what a sight,
Flowers frolic in pure delight.
With laughter and cheer, they make their stand,
In a rhapsody bright, hand in hand!

Between Petal and Blade

There’s a hungry bug on a shiny leaf,
Pulling a prank, what a thief!
Insects giggle, playing hide and seek,
While roses complain, 'We're feeling weak!'

Blades of grass are sharp with wit,
Snapping jokes, they never quit.
Butterflies dance with grace and flair,
While tulips shout, 'We need fresh air!'

Dandelions are the clowns of the field,
Blowing wishes, never concealed.
The sun rolls by with a chuckling sound,
While petals scrunch up, 'Why come around?'

Life's a circus, with nature's jest,
In the wild, we’re always impressed.
Between petal and blade, we find our art,
In laughter and bloom, it's a joyful heart!

The Color of Spring's Breath

Spring sneezes and blooms explode,
Colors splatter on nature’s road.
Buds bursting with giggles and cheer,
While tulips shout, 'Hey, springtime's here!'

A paradox of petals and thorns,
Where laughter mingles with the morn's horns.
Buttercups debate, 'Are we gold or yellow?'
Lilies respond, 'You’re a decent fellow!'

Fragrant whispers fill the air,
As bees dance with a buzzing flair.
Pansies jest, 'We’re the kings of cheer,'
In the color of spring, joy is near!

The daisies nod, ‘Let’s have some fun,’
As tulips race to catch the sun.
In this vibrant ruckus, we find our breath,
In the color of joy, we laugh with depth!

Mosaic of Wild Grows

A mosaic of laughs beneath the sun,
Every bloom here just loves to run.
Daisies giggle in their bright white hats,
While bumblebees dance like silly brats.

Raggedy flowers share the best tales,
Of rogue winds and thunderous gales.
'Can you believe that rain soaked us all?'
'Now look at us, we stand proud and tall!'

Wildflowers whisper secrets so sweet,
Of mischief and pranks, oh so neat.
While daisies laugh, 'We outshined the weeds!'
And every petal rejoices, indeed!

In this garden where laughter sows,
The colors mix, and the wild grows.
A scene so vibrant with joy to bestow,
In the mosaic of life, let's all overflow!

Colors of the Silent Meadow

In a meadow of hues, I tripped on a shoe,
The daisies all giggled; they knew it was true.
A butterfly danced, doing flips in the air,
While I tried to keep up, but my laughter laid bare.

The tulips exclaimed, 'Come join in our spree!',
But the shy daisies waved, saying, 'Not us, you see?'
With each silly step, my socks turned to mud,
And the sunflowers peered as I fell with a thud.

A bumblebee chuckled, on nectar he dined,
His buzzing a tune that was oddly aligned.
While I stood in the green, feeling somewhat amiss,
A whole flock of butterflies offered me bliss.

At the end of the day, as I wiped off my face,
The flowers all winked, 'You've brightened our space!'
And I left the rich land, still giggling with cheer,
For the meadow's great jokes made my troubles unclear.

Echoes of the Orchid

Orchids were gossiping, oh what a scene,
'Have you seen how the roses are acting so mean?'
With whispers and laughter, they stirred in their pots,
Trying to figure out why the daisies wore spots.

A silly old bee gave the orchids a fright,
He buzzed through the petals, then zipped out of sight.
'Are we so attractive, or have we grown loud?'
They shimmied and shook, feeling bold and quite proud.

The violets chimed in, 'Hey, let's throw a ball!
We can dance under stars, just invite one and all!'
But someone suggested to keep it quite small,
To avoid the big roses and their thorns, after all.

So they twirled and they twinkled 'neath the moon's silver glow,
While the crickets joined in with their chirpy show.
And if you heard laughter in echoes that night,
You'd know it was orchids, all partying right!

Garden of Lost Petals

In the garden, a ruckus, petals blew by,
A flower sought safety; it let out a sigh.
With a giggle, a tulip said, 'Oh, what a plight,
Those roses can’t bloom when they’re scared of the height!'

A sunflower chuckled, brushing off dirt,
'That’s just how it goes when you're stuck in a skirt!'
As petals had stories, some swirled in the breeze,
The lilacs just laughed; they were cool as you please.

And who forgot water? The poppies demanded,
But the clematis shrugged, knowing life’s unplanned.
With worms doing salsa, the daisies just bloomed,
Creating a spectacle; oh how they consumed!

From laughter and light, a camaraderie grew,
In the garden of lost, not a tear was in view.
For amidst all the chaos, they found joy in the mess,
In petals and giggles, a grand floral jest.

In the Shade of Cherry Blossoms

Beneath cherry trees, where the sweets often fall,
A squirrel named Nutty claimed he was quite small.
He danced on a branch, then leaped with a flair,
And a petal flew down to get stuck in his hair.

The blossoms all chuckled, 'What's this furry guy?',
As Nutty complained, “I can’t see, oh my!”
With petals like confetti, they twirled in delight,
While the birds high above threw a mini pillow fight.

The breeze played a tune, like a jig in the air,
While rabbits and sparrows joined in with their dare.
Nutty spun ‘round, thinking he was a star,
Until he tripped over blossoms – oh, what a bazaar!

In giggles and blooms, the day turned to dusk,
A tale of the cherry trees, fun, sweet, and brusque.
For life in the shade, with a wink and a jest,
Became one of the best, in a flower-clad fest.

Journey Through Petal Paths

In the garden, weeds do dance,
With silly moves, they take a chance.
A dandelion's wish, stray as can be,
Balloons of fluff on a frolic spree.

Sunflowers laugh, towering proud,
Telling secrets to the passing crowd.
'Why don't roses learn to sing?'
'They'd be the life of every fling!'

Insects buzzing, making jokes,
A bumblebee with playful pokes.
'Tis but a bud, what took so long?'
'Frogs have all the time, and a catchy song!'

Oh, petals twirl in bright delight,
As butterflies plan a moonlit sight.
A daisy shouts, "Join the parade!"
While violets chuckle in leafy shade.

Blooming Curiosity

Petals peek from their cozy beds,
Whispering dreams of butterfly threads.
'What if we wore hats, oh so bright?'
Daisies giggle at the silly sight.

Tulips trip on an afternoon breeze,
As buzzing bees tease with sweet, sticky cheese.
'Can flowers really hit the high notes?'
'Of course, just watch the poppies rock boats!'

The garden sprouts tales, quite absurd,
With ladybugs feasting on scented word.
'Why don't we make a flower stew?'
'Just add some sunshine, and a dash of dew!'

In this patch of painted cheer,
Laughter blooms, year after year.
So let's twirl with petals and grace,
And share a smile with every face!

In the Eye of the Rose

A rose once winked with a cheeky grin,
'Why blend in when you can make a din?'
Petals plumped with stories to share,
While thorns threw sass from their prickly lair.

Lilies lounge in the midday sun,
Sporting shades, they think it’s fun.
'Why not a feast, with birds on the menu?'
'Last time they feasted, we lost our venue!'

In the midst of the buzzing crew,
A sunflower shouts, 'I need a view!'
Decked in humor, they start to sway,
As the garden hosts a lively ballet.

Petunia giggles with pastel flair,
While daisies watch, without a care.
'Next time, let’s try a sassy tango!'
And laugh as ants steal the show, oh no!

Reverberations of Garden Grace

Amidst the blooms, a chorus rings,
Of bee hums and flower flings.
'Why are daisies so darn cute?'
'Because they totally rock the fruit!'

With chatter loud, the garden jives,
In leafy suits, the funthrives.
'Can we throw a prom for pollen pals?'
Yes, let’s dance with the fox and gals!

Petals pirouette with joyful glee,
As bunnies bounce like it's free TV.
'Let’s bake a cake with nectar sweet!'
'Add a sprinkle of laughter, and we can’t be beat!'

As the sun dips low, paints shadows long,
In this garden, the funny stays strong.
With giggles echoing through the air,
Each flower’s joy is a quirky affair.

Tides of Flora

A tulip tried to dive, oh so spry,
But instead it fell, and gave a sigh.
The daisies laughed, they waved their heads,
"Next time, dear tulip, stay out of the beds!"

The roses thought it quite unfair,
To have such drama without a care.
They tossed around their thorns with glee,
And formed a conga line, just wait and see!

Dandelions, bold, blew seeds like dreams,
Creating mustaches with their wild schemes.
But one got tangled, what a sight!
A hairy sunflower, oh what a fright!

In this garden of whimsy, all’s not so fair,
But laughter blooms freely, floating in air.
With petals and giggles spread all around,
A party of plants, now that's profound!

A Symphony of Marred Beauty

In a concert hall made of wilting petals,
A beetle played tunes with his tiny kettles.
He missed the beat, and flew with a clank,
The daisies joined in, said, "Give us a rank!"

A rose took the mic, with thorns shining bright,
She crooned a ballad deep into the night.
But her high note slipped, and bees buzzed away,
"Retire the mic! It's now time to play!"

Orchids shook their heads, "What a mess! What a show!"

As their neighbor, a lily, wore a straw bow.
They danced on stage while petals flew 'round,
Making wigs out of blossoms to the funky sound!

So join in the fun, find your flower groove,
Let laughter break through, see how you move.
In this colorful symphony, there's no right or wrong,
Just a chorus of blooms, singing silly songs!

Petals on the Wind

A petals' dance upon a breeze,
They twirled and spun, as if to tease.
One landed in a cat's fuzzy ear,
The feline meowed, "What's this? Oh dear!"

Winds kicked up a flower fight,
As blossoms pelted with pure delight.
The sunflowers laughed, tall and proud,
While pansies formed a giggling crowd.

A butterfly slipped, all feathers and grace,
But she stumbled and fell on a flower's face.
"Watch where you're fluttering!" shouted a rose,
"Your wings are a mess, goodness knows!"

Yet in this garden, chaos was king,
With giggles and petals, what joy they bring.
So catch a wild petal if you're feeling bold,
And let the wind's whimsy wrap you like gold!

Whispered Blossoms

Two blooms whispered secrets under the sun,
"Have you heard the rumors? It's just begun!"
A daffodil fished for juicy tales,
While a shy pansy giggled, her laughter pales.

The lilacs turned purple with envy and cheer,
As the gossip spread wide for all blooms to hear.
"Did you see the tulip in that silly hat?"
"Fashion faux pas," said a curious cat.

Their whispers floated, tickling the bees,
Who buzzed with excitement, "Oh please! Oh please!"
Hearing all the tales made their work quite divine,
They spread the sweet nectar, how perfectly fine!

In gardens full of chatter, laughter ignites,
Petals tell stories of whimsical sights.
So join the discussion, don't muss up the plot,
In the realm of blossoms, it's all worth a shot!

Petals in the Breeze

Petals dance in the air,
Like birds without a care.
They swirl and twirl around,
Chasing giggles on the ground.

Sunflowers grin wide and bright,
Winking at the morning light.
Tulips blush as bees go by,
Silly hats on flowers high.

Daisies play a game of tag,
While roses wear a fancy rag.
Laughter spreads from bud to bud,
As violets tease in the mud.

Jolly pansies pause to laugh,
Telling jokes on the green path.
Nature’s chatters, light and free,
A garden's giggle, can't you see?

Whispers of Blossoms

Blossoms gossip in the breeze,
Mumbling secrets with such ease.
Zinnias chuckle, petals wide,
While lilies strut with floral pride.

Dandies make the best of shows,
Tickling bees on tiny toes.
Petunias plan a grand parade,
With bumblebees as their aid.

Sun-kissed daisies lift their heads,
Imagining their flower beds.
A wisteria with twisted grin,
Says, "Hold on, let the fun begin!"

Amidst the bloom, a joke unfolds,
Stories of dirt and sun that mold.
In this garden, laughter thrives,
Among the blooms, the joy derives!

Frayed Bloom

One petal's hanging by a thread,
A daisy dreams of all that's said.
"Oh, how I wish to stay in bloom!"
Yet naps in sun are none too gloom.

The tulips burst with vibrant hues,
While daisies wear mismatched shoes.
Critters giggle through the grass,
As flowers prance, say, "Let it pass!"

Charmed by butterflies' ballet,
Petals laugh and sway and play.
A frayed bloom has seen it all,
With stories made to make us fall.

Clicking beetles in a line,
Join the show, they toe the line.
In this patch, it's all a scheme,
To wake up and just share their dream!

Fragments of Garden Dreams

A quirky sprout with crazy hair,
Whispers tales of summer fare.
Roses wear their socks askew,
And daisies giggle at the view.

Buttercups toss their heads with glee,
As busy ants run wild and free.
A sunflower jokes about the sun,
"I'm just here to have some fun!"

The violets play a silly game,
With daffodils all shouting names.
Everyone's a little wild,
In this dream, we're all but styled.

As night falls, the stars all smile,
Garden blooms will rest awhile.
With laughter echoing in their seams,
Tomorrow brings more garden dreams!

Where Butterflies Converse

In a meadow bright, they flap and twirl,
Whispering secrets with a dancing swirl.
They gossip on petals, a colorful stage,
Wings all aflutter, they're the life of the page.

With nectar for tea, they sip and they share,
Laughing at bees caught in floral despair.
'You missed the best bloom!' one butterfly cries,
As another lands softly, with a wink from its eyes.

A ladybug rolls, pretending to snooze,
But secretly dreams of amazing flower views.
They plan grand romances under the sun,
While swapping some gossip, oh what fun!

As shadows grow long, they bid their adieu,
Bidding farewell to the sky's brilliant blue.
In whispers they promise to meet here again,
Where flowers are friends, and laughter is zen.

The Secret Life of Stems

In the garden below, what a sight to behold,
Stems share their stories, both silly and bold.
They giggle and wiggle, try not to fall,
As they wait for their flowers to straighten up tall.

Bending and swaying, they form quite a crew,
Pass around jokes like a botanical brew.
A twig tells a tale about a squirrel named Ned,
Who mistook a sunflower for his cozy bed.

One stem even boasts of a bee's wild flight,
That danced through the blossoms from morning till night.

They cheer for their blooms, with petals so bright,
Rooting for greatness, oh what a delight!

At twilight they settle, in hours of calm,
Imagining rainbows and sweet morning balm.
With laughter and joy, they sway side to side,
In the secret realm where their dreams coincide.

Gypsy Garden Dreams

In a wild patch of green, with colors so bright,
Gypsies of petals laugh under moonlight.
They spin and they twirl, oh what a show,
Waving to dandelions that tumble and blow.

With wishes a'whirl, the daisies all plot,
To paint all the night with ideas they've got.
While tulips in ruffles spill tea by the pond,
Sharing wild stories of the dreams they respond.

Violets tiptoe, with secrets to keep,
Whispering loudly while the night creatures sleep.
Roses serenade with a whimsical tune,
While geraniums sway to the light of the moon.

They dance through the shadows, as laughs take their flight,
In a gypsy-descend of a whimsical night.
Garden of laughter, a carousel bright,
Where petals unite in a dreamy delight.

Wilted Wishes

Oh, the sad little daisies, with heads hung so low,
They can’t find their sparkle or the sunshine’s glow.
With donuts of dew and soggy old dreams,
They laugh at the daisies’ wilted extremes.

‘What’s the secret?’ one posy asked with a sigh,
‘To bloom and to flourish, oh me, oh my!'
The lily replied with a cheerful cheer,
‘Just sip on the sunshine and dance without fear!’

A tulip piped up, ‘We’ll weather this storm,
Let’s laugh at our fates; it’s how we transform!’
With giggles and wiggles, they sparked a delight,
Sprouting new dreams in the soft, gentle night.

As pollen drifts by, they jive with the breeze,
For wishes don’t wilt when you smile with ease.
With petals all worn, they still share a grin,
And cherish their laughter, that’s where life begins.

www.ingramcontent.com/pod-product-compliance
Lightning Source LLC
Chambersburg PA
CBHW071840160426
43209CB00003B/366
* 9 7 8 1 8 0 5 6 6 7 0 1 8 *